T0194084

ALCAN HIGHWAY TO

Alaska

A TRIP IN 1968 DURING THE AGE OF AQUARIUS

VALENTINE L. KRUMPLIS

Trafford rev. 04/06/2020

 www.trafford.com

North America & international
toll-free: 1 888 232 4444 (USA & Canada)
fax: 812 355 4082

Foreword

That year 1968 was the peak of a revolution, a change in our culture that threw away the final constraints of the stifling 1950's. It was the beginning of the end of racism, sexism and all kinds of prejudices that had clouded the minds of people for generations. Most noticeable at our age was the casting off sexual repression that had been implanted on young people by the religious fanatics, the withered old nuns and the perverted priests.

What brought this beautiful people movement is hard to figure out. Was it the pill? Was it the drugs? LSD... the so called Acid? Was it the anti-war feeling? Our culture opened up like a blooming flower to show all the beauty of the human spirit. The Age of Aquarius was here in 1968. We planned to do a little bit of everything, hunt wolves, pan for gold, meet a lot of girls, and do sight seeing, take a lot of photographs.

We decided to quit our jobs and travel the Alcan Highway all 1200 miles of gravel looking for all kinds of adventure. We did not know a lot about hunting wolves for a bounty or how and where to pan for gold.

The changes at that time were eye popping. The long hair on young men shattered the long accepted haircuts and frightened the older generation. The kids looked like Russian Bolsheviks, they talked of free love, living in communes and wore outlandish clothes. They painted their vans, busses and cars in weird colors. These new young people were called hippies. The girls dressed provocatively displaying tits and asses. It was a grand time to be young.

1968......... A YEAR OF A CULTURAL EXPLOSION, AND OUR DECISION TO DRIVE THE ALCAN HIGHWAY TO ALASKA

About The Author...
His Mind Set

I, having gone to a catholic grammar school and an all boys Catholic high school, I was truly the best example of a sexually, religiously repressed victim of that old religious culture. I still believed that masturbating or missing mass on Sunday would send a person to hell for all eternity. The cultural religious strangle hold that nuns and priests had on young people can not be understood or described, you had to have lived it to understand it.

So ...the liberating feelings that 1968 gave people frightened the older generations but gave energy to the young to wake up and live. This is probably why we decided to stop working, saving, and then throwing off all constraints and going to Alaska. We really, really did what most people dream of doing and never do it.

THE MAIN CHARACTERS ON THE ALCAN TRIP WALLY AND VAL

WALLY...

How do you describe a friend? Wally was a tall, thin guy, twenty six years old, he still is tall and thin 50 years later. He has an accounting degree from University of Illinois, Urbana. Wally always had good jobs and dabbled in the stock market. He knew how to save money and build up wealth. He was an avid hunter and fisherman and a very good shooter…so a great guy to travel with to Alaska.

VAL…

I was 27 years old at that great time (Can you believe I am writing about this trip 50 years later…that has to be a little crazy?).

This is how I looked 50 years ago on our trip.

I had a BS degree in marketing/advertising from the University of Illinois in Urbana. I had the best job I was a marketing representative for Charmin Paper Co. I was selling toilet paper, Charmin, White cloud, Puffs tissues, and Bounty towels. People that wanted to put me down would just say I was an ass wipe paper salesman, however it was the best job anyone could have. There were no hours that could be regulated or checked, there were no managers during the day.

The products were in the stores already all we had to do is get the stores to promote them in their weekly ads. We made sure our products were priced right and had proper space on the shelf.

THERE WERE SOME NEGATIVE IMAGES ABOUT MARKETING TOILET PAPER

My poor aunt came to my mother one day and said, "Val go to college for 4 years now he sells toilet paper door to door" My mother tried to explain and justify my career choice.

To put that job problem to rest I have to say that the job was the best anyone could have. I had a company car, two months bonus every year, good salary and could work as many hours a day I wanted. There was no way the management could check how much we worked. We could work 2-3 hours a day or work 6 hours a day, it was impossible to keep track on us. I took full advantage of the flexible hours and the complete lack of any supervision.

Some on our sales team, fellow salesmen had other jobs, others remodeled their homes, there was no way for the company to check how many hours we worked per day. There are no jobs like that today and there will never be a time where the workers can get away with working less.

I was always visiting my girlfriend during the day when I chose to work the short hours, this was truly a lot of fun and a great benefit for me.

My girl friend.

I had a lot of free time and energy so I decided to sell the store owners on allowing me to put in some vending machines in their stores. I started setting up gumball machines in the stores. I would fill the machines on Saturdays and split the profits with the store. I would get fifteen dollars in pennies when machine was empty and then give the store five and keep five. It would cost me five to fill the machine. The great part of this venture was that I was also a coin collector and found many good coins in my machines. I had penny, nickel and dime machines.

So...why quit a job like that? Why stop visiting my beautiful girlfriend any day during the week? Why? Why? The answer perhaps was that I was not challenged enough. I felt somehow that I had to do something greater, bigger, and much more meaningful.

Is it some human trait to get bored when everything seems to be going well? I was drinking way too much at that time. It was party after party and it seems I did not know how to have fun without drinking. The people of the Lithuanian/American Community drank a lot, most of it was hard liqueur.

My drinking began to show some physical symptoms, the whites of my eyes started to look yellow, brown spots on my chest started appearing, liver seemed swollen. These symptoms caused me to go visit my family Dr. Adomavicius who examined me and when I went back to hear about my tests the good doctor really, really, surprised me. He said Krumpliali, Krumpliali, a diminutive use of my last name, get a gun and shoot yourself. What a prognosis of my symptoms. I am sure no one else ever got told that by any other doctor. The good doctor explained that my liver was partially destroyed from heavy drinking and in a few years I would die a horrible death. He said I would make my family suffer and I would suffer... so save everyone the pain of a long lingering death, and I should go and shoot myself. This doctor was weird but his advice had the perfect effect on me...I stopped drinking immediately. Maybe that knowledge that I was near death if I kept drinking triggered in me the desire to quit everything and go to Alaska?

The good doctor also explained that people can live on one sixteenth of their liver if they stop drinking. Ok, ok, I stopped drinking but how do I continue having fun at parties without booze? Easy answer Val...smoke grass and get silly, have fun at parties, do that and keep up with all of your boozed up friends.

So...no more booze, eyes got white and I was a happy partygoer again.

My personal relationship also seemed to have hit a bump. I had been dating the same girl for four years and got engaged to her but it did not seem a perfect match. I believed we both felt the same way. She wanted to travel to Europe and I wanted my adventure in Alaska. So... to this day I hope I did not hurt her feelings as we seemed to drift apart.

Planning for Our Trip

We figured we would probably be gone a couple of months. I had to give up my company car and so we had to plan our trip from square one. I had a 1960 Austin Healey bug eyed Sprite, definitely a useless car for an Alaska trip Wally had a 1966 Volkswagen and that was selected over the Austin Healey. The VW could not fit all of our stuff and we could not sleep in it or on it.

It was his car and so I went out and bought a used Montgomery Ward Pop Up tent camper/trailer, I do not remember what I paid for it, maybe about $500. The trailer was low and was just a rectangular metal box measuring about 8x6 feet and the top was made up of two beds for sleeping that were slid out to the sides. A tent covered the camper when the beds were positioned to the sides. I have included several pictures of camper. You can see how compact it is when prepped for travel and how it looks set up for sleeping. There was space on the floor of the camper for our guns and camping gear.

See pictures in book of camper in travel mode and in camping mode.

Our gear, our stuff we packed it all in, we had so much stuff. First we had all our guns, rifles and shotguns, a bow with arrows and I even had a 9 mm. Luger pistol, knives, fishing rods and reels, cooking utensils, cameras-35 mm and a film camera. We had sleeping bags, pillows and a good selection of hunting clothes and rain gear. So... one could say we had a lot of stuff. We also took a good quantity of grass because I had given up drinking. We were prepared to hunt, explore, cook what we shot or caught and photo our adventure with many pictures. I took some travel checks, Wally had several credit cards, so...we were well set up for cash and credit.

We had read about the snow melt and the Alcan road problems in spring so we waited until mid June to leave on our trip. I had lied to my company I worked for saying I was waiting for some liver tests to be sent to me. So...I was partially on sick leave and or vacation.

My two problems complicating my Alaska trip were that I was breaking up with the girl I was engaged with but that seemed was a mutual perception of our relationship going nowhere. My problem number two was that I was living with my mother who did not want me to go on this adventure. My mother was collecting disability but she also had some savings to go on living in our rented apartment. So...there was no problem that I was abandoning a sickly parent with no subsistence ability. This was one of the few times I resisted my mother's wishes and told her I was going. This was a bit emotional for me because in my own way I loved my mother and we were friends. My mother was still getting over my father's death in January of 1967, he died of a heart problem when he was 55 years old.

So...one fine morning in June 14, 1968 we hooked up the Montgomery Ward Camper and started driving. Our plan was to drive through the states of Wisconsin and Minnesota

We took turns driving but that became a problem...not to me but to my friend Walter. The VW had a speedometer screen marked off with some indicating lines when to shift to a higher gear. It seemed to Walter that I was shifting too late or to early and that was ruining his transmission.

Walter sat there for miles in anguish watching me shift the wrong way…a little too late or a little too early.

Anyway that is the way the trip started. To overcome my problem of shifting Wally drove most of the 12,000 miles we put on his VW.

I also kept a diary if you can imagine it is now 50 years old. I will print up material from the diary that will be con current with some of my story. I will differentiate it by the italic script.

From Diary

> *6/14-15, 1968*
> *Wisc. Dells, Fishermans Luck Camp*
>
> *Good weather, bright-sunny, not so hot. Mosquitos are biting very bad*
> *Last night set up camp and went into town after a few puffs. The town was still very dead.*
> *Woke up at dawn but got up at 8:30 and went fishing. Walter said I would not catch any fish-but I did catch a 21 inch/2 lb. sheep head that we cleaned and had for breakfast.*
> *Walter did not catch anything (small bass 11 in.) except he took off his pants and went into the river to get a 69 cent lure.*
> *Thinking about pussy-nice warm little pussy.*
> *Made cold beet soup.*
>
> *Mileage was 37730 morning-----38000 night.*

pictures of our first camp

We survived our first day of the journey and managed to set up our camper and prepare food. According to my diary we drove 270 miles. The car is working the camper can be set up for sleeping…so all seems okay.

It also seems that I was fixated on pussy because out of nowhere the last sentence of that day in my diary mentions pussy. It also seems insane that embarking on this great trip I would be fixated on that. I think that being at our age this fixation on pussy is a driving force for all young humans. This fixation or hormonal influence colors our whole trip. Today as I look back 50 years it seems ridiculous to be so influenced by sex. That force was very powerful when you were in your twenties.

Today I can not understand the religious obsession of trying to suppress that force for several thousand years. Making all sex forbidden and a sin, and then imposing celibacy on the religious orders, this is an enigma that something so powerful and great as sex would be constantly forbidden.

This suppression of sex was the culture of the past and in 1968 we seem to break out of that repression.

On June 16, 1968 we started out with the odometer reading 38,000 miles. I will now put in the diary notes for that day.

> *6/16/68*
> *Minnesota, N. Dakota, Saskatchewan.*
> *Weather…Partly sunny-partly rain.*
>
> *"Ass in Saskatchewan" Lucky Pierre started out early in the morning and crossed Minnesota and N. Dakota and camped 13 miles in Saskatchewan, Canada.*
> *Declared my Luger pistol and smuggled in some pot in my boots. Here we met an old Swede who told us about Alaska. Lucky Pierre is afraid of 1000 miles of gravel road. Stopped for tea and met Elsa the 17 yr. old waitress…tried to get her to come to our party-but no-she almost agreed- would have been a very nice young piece of ass. Took a walk in N.D. Hills found a fox den with*

some fox shit. Looking forward to meeting some girls in Saskatchewan.

Odometer reading at night was 38,591 (so we had driven 591 miles)

As our travel begins you can see our thinking is very one tracked, we are obsessed by the sexual drive. How hard was it for the past two thousand years for the leaders of the world not to see this driving force and try to figure out ways to guide that force in a beneficial way. That was not to be, rationality was ignored and that drive was declared instead a gift from the gods, it was declared a sin and humanity was punished for a natural instinct.

I really am getting away from a travelogue and ranting...so...let us go to June 17, 1968

Walter standing by Alaska Highway sign

Saskatchewan
Odometer reading morning 38591

This morning we woke up and missed a chance to make friends with a very friendly middle aged woman. We drove across Saskatchewan and found a dead raccoon— we stopped and cut of its tail. We stopped in Regina, Saskatchewan, and met two very nice girls Jennifer and Margie. They shoved us some parks and a museum took some pictures. Very nice girls. We stopped and shot bow and arrows. We camped in Saskatoon, could not pick up girls.

I forgot to mention that at the Canadian border I had to state that I had a Luger pistol and that the Canadians permitted me to bring it across Canada if I would put it in a plastic baggie and had the baggie sealed with a lead seal. So... if I broke the seal before reaching the Canadian / Alaska border I would be in violation. This was weird to me because if I was a bad person I would use the Luger and then throw it away. It was strange to have my luger in a plastic baggie, but it made the Canadians feel safer.

Odometer reading at night was 38, 922

Pictures in Regina. Pictures of Jennifer and Margie

Pictures in Museum…Val and the girls

Picture of our camp in Saskatoon.

6/18//68
Saskatoon
Sunny and Warm.

Organized our stuff in the morning, then I called the assholes in Chicago (P.G.). I have made up my mind that I would like to teach.

Then we met a very nice girl Shirly Jacharias, following this we went to a hippy house and found out that we missed a hippy girl that would have gone to Alaska with us by 4 hours.

Edmonton-camped in city campsite. Went to Zorbas Discothec to look for cook. Met several girls, Norma was slightly interested in going with us.

Morning odometer was 38922 --- night was39,305

(so...we had driven 383 miles)

is a picture of a Match book from Zorbas Discotheque giving their phone and address.

Is me by a sign of …Province of Alberta

me looking at the landscape---maybe?

Edmonton, Alberta seemed that it was the start of that Alcan Highway. We were there June 19, 1968. We never realized that what 1200 miles of gravel road was. The gravel road was destructive on our small trailer tires. Every hundred miles you could see the wear on the small tires. The gas stations along the highway were aware of how fast little tires got chewed up, so...they had a large supply of little tires to sell. We kept buying the little tires.

From the diary.

> *6/19/68*
> *Edmonton, Alberta*
> *Weather...Cloudy...70's*
>
> *Horny....*
>
>> *Found a dead female moose and saw a deer.*
>> *Pulled into Grand Prairie. Met an old man in a café by noticing his silver dollar and introduced us to Louis Garskie, famous, rich gold miner. They showed us their gold and gold buttons, wolf and fox hides, pistols and jade. Very friendly– they asked us about what we did and what we owned (a little too curious). After leaving them and smoking some pot...we began to suspect that they were thieves and killers–so...we reported them to the R.C.M.P. I was afraid that they will shoot us so I loaded my gun that night.*
>>
>> *Odometer morning was 39305..........night was 39719*

Our Stop at Grande Prairie was one filled with many strange memories. Right around Edmonton we drove by a dead moose. The moose was hit by a car and you could see a whole ton of car parts around the dead moose. I am sure the car had to be towed away. This was a good warning for us not to hit animals crossing in front of us.

.... The dead moose

......See deer

After finishing breakfast we went to pay by the register and there I found an old guy paying for his coffee with a silver dollar. So, I say to him...can I buy the silver dollar and give you a paper dollar. We make the deal and introduce ourselves.

His old man says he lives in a trailer with Louie Garskie the famous gold miner and we can go to the trailer and meet him.

Louie is a friendly old guy and shows off his gold. The gold is like pieces of rice he has stored in some soda bottles, it is very impressive. Louie also shows us gold buttons he has cast and wants us to buy some. Louie then tries to sell us a huge tanned wolf skin, taller than a six foot man. He then shows us a German luger with a long barrel, the type used by tank crews. We like everything but have a budget for traveling so we do not buy anything.

The two old guys seem very curious about us and ask us what we have with us and is anyone expecting us in Alaska. The questions seem strange to me. As we part Louie gives each of us a stone with a gold vein in it, I still have mine. Louie also gives me a postcard about him.

..........Louie Garskie panning gold ....

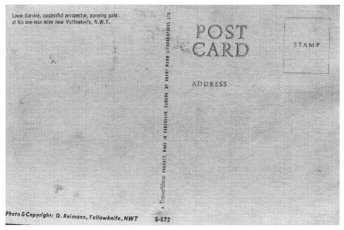

Louie Garskie, successful prospector, panning gold at his one-man mine near Yellowknife, N.W.T.

POST CARD

ADDRESS

STAMP

Photo & Copyright: G. Reimann, Yellowknife, NWT   S-572

..........Back of card with verbiage about Louie.

Back in our camp, I smoke a lot of pot. And become very suspicious of our encounter with the two old guys. I think I am paranoid. I start believing the two old guys are thieves and killers. This paranoia continues for a few days. I am convinced the two old guys want to kill us. So...when I go to sleep I load my shotgun and rifle and pack my bags of clothes along the tent wall by my bed. I am convinced that they will put in rattle snakes in our camper. I do not let Walter go into the camper until I do a search with a stick. When we are driving I am convinced they will shoot Walter first and I will have a gun battle by myself.

The paranoia persists as I keep smoking my pot. The long drive on the road see picture of boring long road.

lonely road

The culmination of the paranoia is reached when I insist on reporting my suspicions to the R.C.M.P. Walter can not believe I will do that, he thinks I am really crazy.

Picture of our car and camper and me reporting my suspicions about the Louie Garskie gang.

I told the officers that the Garskie gang might kill us and that if that happens they should have my report. The officers listened politely and wrote something up.

This was the last straw for Walter and he told me he can not stand my paranoia anymore and if I keep smoking we are turning around and going home. I stopped smoking and it took about three days for me to start thinking normally.

This episode was a weird event in our trip and in my life. I can not believe how chemicals and drugs can make you completely nuts. My lesson was a very good warning to stay away from acid and other mind altering chemicals.

June 20, 1968
Place...Bunnys Lodge
Weather.....Partly sunny, cloudy

Went to Fort St. John bought supplies, trap, gold pan, Called Metcalf (my boss at P.G.) ----I am healthy---good. (I had been waiting for some medical reports)

Went back and forth past a group of Indians trying to decide if we should camp at Sikini River where we saw some real nice girls.

Odometer reading morn. 39,719...night 39,978

Pictures by Sikini River camp.... Walter by our camper.

I do not remember what kind of trap I bought at Fort St. John but I still have the gold panning pan we used for panning for gold. It is just a large metal soup dish.

…. Me panning for gold by a river holding the panning dish.

We also camped along some side roads when we did not get to a town.

….Me by camper.

…..Walter by camper

Fort St. John put us in British Columbia I think we began to notice that it almost never gets dark at night. As we drive along we notice in British Columbia and the Yukon that we come across some small farms, homesteads and little stores...these are the true pioneers in this area. I think they received some free acres to homestead and develop. So...here they are mostly young couples trying to survive in this bitter land. The land they own is by the side of the road and most of it is covered by muskeg... (Muskeg—description...Muskeg is an acidic soil type common in Arctic and boreal areas, although it is found in other northern climates as well. Muskeg is Approximately synonymous with bogland, but "muskeg" is the standard term in Western Canada and Alaska, while "bog" is common elsewhere). Wikipedia

Must of the people we see living along the road are young couples. They subsist on hunting and fishing. I look at their property covered with muskeg and I see the impossibility of clearing this land by hand. You have to get to the dirt I believe to be able to grow something. To clear the muskeg I think would take some big equipment and a lot of money which the homesteaders did not have.

Walter by one of the stores along the highway

June 21,1968
Place....Muncho lake

Weather So, so

Early morning Wally spotted a missing nut on our trailer, so we had to do a little repair work at a standard station. Our lantern is also on the bum. Driving along we got a flat tire on the trailer and found out that our flat can not be fixed so we bought a new tire. Stopped in Fort Nelson and met a nice part indian Girl who might have taken up with us if it were not for her boyfriend. Camped at Muncho Lake. I made some hamburgers that Wally says taste like shit. Wally's sex drive is diminished today for girl chasing.

Odometer reading morning 39,978.....Night 40,179

.......Muncho Lake

.......Walter on a mountain

........Val on mountain.

.........Val looking at the 1200 mile road

............Dust on road

We are now in the mountains. The road is still dirt and gravel. We can only drive about 30 miles per hour because of the many twists and turns on this shit road. Seldom, if you ever meet other cars on this road. No one ever passes you. The dust raised by an approaching car is horrible…it blinds you.

Along the way we run into a very interesting event. It was getting late in the day and we were looking for a place to pull over and set up camp. As we drove along we saw a car with its hood up along the road and two women waving for us to stop. We stopped to help them out. They were in their mid thirties and average looking in good shape. They also wore dresses that showed a quantity of tit. We, forgot the tits and were concerned about the car problem and how to help them. Wally started looking at the engine and I got into the car and turned the key...well, would you now it, the car started and kept running. We felt so proud of ourselves at being good mechanics that nothing else entered our minds. The women thanked us and we got into our car and drove off. Their car was facing the direction we were coming from. We drove for about a half hour when I said, "You know I think there was nothing wrong with the car, the women were just looking to camp with someone for the night." So now we feel like Dumb and Dumber. Wally says "They were showing a lot of very good tit." We had to have been so stupid. We could have stayed with them and who knows what would have happened at night? Now we start calculating how far they have gone in the opposite direction and how long would it take to go back. It is impossible to catch them because you can not speed on this gravel road. The realization that we passed up some possible sex hits us very hard.

It is me with a marmot I shot on a mountain.

It is me on a snow cowered mountain.

I am checking out our trailer in the mountains

People always talk about cabin fewer...after being in a VW on a gravel road at 30 miles per hour, I can tell you there is such thing as small car fewer. You see one mountain then another and another and you begin to not be impressed by the vistas.

Another mountain

Val on mountain with car and camper below

Meeting someone on the road is always exiting.

A car approaching with a dust cloud.

Someone driving in front. We can not get close. You can also see on the sides of the road the most boring views

June 22, 1968
Out of Muncho Lake

> *Weather....Rainy*
> *We had an oil change at mile 40175*
> *Trailer broke down for the third time.*
> *Two women with broken car tried to meet us—but we were like assholes and did not realize that they might want to camp and fuck with us.*

> *Millage*
> *Morn 40179 night 40564*

June 23, 1968
White horse

> *Weather....good, warm*
> *Pulled into White Horse to take showers and wash our clothes.*
> *Met a nice family with a nice daughter at a chicken place. Family seemed interested in having us hang around the daughter.*
> *Tried to pick up two girl hitch-hikers. I used the Yukon approach (tough). "You wanna come along with us?" We got turned down. Made camp at Sulfur Lake.*

> *Morning....40564 night....40778*

My travelogue gets into trouble because I stop posting every day and combine a post from June 24-June 30

Anyway here is the long post: It contains our trip through the Yukon into Alaska and then back through the Yukon and British Columbia.

Yes...sorry to have left of for so long.

Val by the Yukon sign

Val Standing by Alaska Sign

We crossed the border into Alaska and there were no border agents, Canadian or American to report to. My pistol was still in the plastic bag sealed with the lead seal. We never went deeper into Alaska, we stayed near the border with our hunting and gold panning. If you look at the map you can see a town called Chicken and that is were we hung around.

We camped out on Taylor highway in Alaska. We spent a few days hunting bear and wolf. I also shot a porcupine with my 30-06 and one with buckshot.(I have to interject here and say I am against wanton killing---I really, really was going to cook and eat them…but that did not happen because they smelled like pine) We searched the mountains and valleys for bear but we did not find any bear signs anywhere. We found bear tracks but did not know how old they were. One night while driving on Taylor highway we saw a wolf-we chased it through the woods. From then on we hunted wolf at night from the car. We took the passenger seat out and Wally drove while I sat in the back and was prepared to shoot wolf out of the open sun roof. During the days we hunted for bear.

We broke camp and went up further north along Taylor highway where we found a campsite along Wade Creek (Gold). We hunted from here for several days between Wade Creek and Mosquito river for bear and Mosquito River and Fair Play mountain for wolf.

At this campsite we met an old man traveling by himself from Mesa, Colorado a (Rick Biser). We called him Colorado and enjoyed his company very much.

I went panning for gold with him and we worked a bunch of streams ripping apart some bedrock flat rocks from the bottom of the streams. But found no color. Next day Colorado found a gold nugget.

We parted company with Colorado and drove north toward Chicken, Alaska. We passed Chicken and never knew about it. I think Chicken had one store and two houses.

So… our stay in Alaska was not that long. In our conversations with Colorado we learned a lot about panning for gold. First you have to find a stream that shows some color in the gravel. You try to pick up gravel from the lowest areas because gold is heavy. You rip up the flat rocks on the bottom and scoop up the gravel and you do all this in freezing mountain streams all day long. I gave up that plan of getting rich.

Colorado also told us of going upstream till you find a gold vein or source where the stream starts picking up color.

Walter standing I think on a paved road

So…not finding any gold nuggets, not shooting any wolves or seeing black bears we decided to try our luck in California and Mexico. We took a different road south. We crossed the border using highway 9 into Yukon toward Dawson city on the Yukon River.

Walter standing by the Yukon sign

It is humorous today to look at Alaskan hunts with thousands of dollars worth of equipment and expensive guides, special camouflage clothes, four wheelers, tents, horses, cooks, guides and all of that…we had nothing but ourselves, see pictures 34 and 35. We had fun and did not feel for a moment we needed any extra stuff. We were free, young and looking for adventure.

Val with rifle hunting

Walter with rifle hunting.

Val up in the high country checking out snow

Val in the high country holding a 9mm luger pistol

Crossing back into Yukon no one checked us out for anything. A few miles into Yukon we came up to the Yukon River and had to load up and take the ferry across. Everything is so well organized that you can just enjoy the scenery and get to Dawson City when you cross the river.

Crossing Yukon River on the ferry

Getting off the ferry

Walter jumping, celebrating crossing the Yukon River.

Our departure from Alaska was no big event for us, traveling the Alaska Highway was the heart of the adventure. Looking for girls, looking at the scenery, shooting our guns and just having a great time doing everything and nothing, having no deadlines, no tasks, that, was the fun part. I guess being free of obligations, being young that was the key to our being happy. We joked a lot and gave ourselves nick names.

At this point leaving Alaska I will go back to my Fifty year old diary in Italics.

We said goodbye to Colorado (Rich Biser, he was old in 1968) and drove north toward Chicken Alaska. We passed Chicken and never knew it. As we entered the Yukon, "Deadeye Dawson (Walter) shot a marmot and Lucky Pierre (Val) cleaned and stretched the skin for 8 hours in the car.

Walter skinning his marmot

We saw Dawson City on the Yukon River, once a mighty boom town of 40,000 and now only a few miserable souls wander through the aging, leaning deserted houses and old bars.

I gave a sermon to two people from the rotten steps of St. Andrews condemned Church.

Abandoned church I Dawson

Ferry on the Yukon River

Walter at the border marker.

We left Dawson without seeing the customs office. (Before we left we had to wake the gas attendant to come from the house and give us gas)

Out of Dawson we had a flat tire. We drove all night till we ran out of gas 1 mile before Carmacks, Yukon. Wally slept and I walked to town where I met (beautiful) Alice who sold me some gas in a milk quart and an empty oil can.

We drove into town and here at the gas station we found out from a teacher that the fishing was great at Tetchin Lake for pike and Frenchman's Lake for trout. We also found out that a black bear, and a grizzly bear come up to Frenchman's Lake to eat fish. Well we bought our fishing licenses and clipped out (oops), we forgot to pull up our jacks on the trailer and bent the two front ones on the trailer. We also set up a party with Alice for the night.

We fished and Wally caught a few pike (7 fish) and one of them was 5 ½ lbs. and 31 inches long. In our camp on

Frenchman's Lake there were other people camping. Here I cleaned the fish and dried my feet for I had been bow fishing with my moccasins on. It takes 2 hours to make a round trip to Carmacks-so Wally left to pick up Alice and I stayed to clean up the fish-lo and behold the black bear came into camp amid all the people and walked around smelling for fish. I took movies of him, gave him fish and shot near him to scare him away.

Wally came back with Alice and Lynn and we fried some pancakes and then went into the camper to have our pot party.

We crawled into our beds and when the lights went out the hanging lantern started moving around. The lantern moved and bounced and the trailer shook. It bounced for me and Wally but not quite for the same reason.

We spent the next few days camping, fishing, loving, and smoking pot.

We also planned to kill the black bear

Our plan was to shoot the bear with my arrow and then if it was not mortally hit Wally would kill it with his gun and then it would be his hide.

The bear came into camp at regular time, 9 am, 12 noon, and 5 pm.

I sharpened my arrows and waited---we were also going to record the kill on a movie camera.

Wally left to pick up the girls and I stayed in camp.

The black bear came around and as I had been planning to wash up I was by the lake. I had my towel, soap, and shotgun. The bear came toward me and I fired two shots, one at a garbage can to scare it but it kept coming toward me, so I backed right into the lake with my shotgun.

The bear walked away and I walked out of the lake, picked up my soap and a garbage cover and this time started washing up, the bear came toward me again and I moved to deeper water and continued washing up.

This time the bear stayed by the shore for about an hour and I almost shit an icicle, it was so cold in that deeper water. I did not shoot the bear because I wanted Wally to be in on the kill.

Well talk got around town that we were camped out there and wanted the bear----so one day as I was walking from the shit house with my shotgun, fishing pole toward the lake...the local cop and a forest service game warden came up in a truck and asked me if the bear had come up. I told them about my experience in the lake with the bear, they laughed and told me that these black bears are very dangerous.

They also told me that it was illegal for me to have my guns out.

Wally pulled up and we talked some more---the more Wally talked, asking them to let us shoot the bear, the more the cops became interested in us.---"We are suspicious". They now asked us to show what guns we own. Here the two grubby looking guys started bringing out six guns, scopes, binoculars, and four cameras. The cops were amazed. The cop asked Wally if he knew how to shoot...gave him his 357 mag. and deadeye almost hit the can.

We now knew we could not shoot the bear anymore so we decided to pull out, and the RCM cop also told us to go to White Horse and register and seal our guns.

We fished one more day and Wally and Lynn caught one fish apiece, and I caught two, one was full of worms and the other was a large pike. I told Wally I caught a 50 lb gar as a joke.

That night we had the biggest pot party I can imagine-----I went into a religious trance and did a wolfman act, then I went to sleep and Wally and Lynn went to bed.

Special Wally Quote

> *"Val had rapport with Alice but at the end he did not want to shake the lantern with her".*

The next day we left Carmacks, Yukon. (trailer had a flat)

As I drove on around mile 778, I went into a turn on a hill and went into a fishtail and flipped our trailer and almost went into a ravine. As we stood there in the middle of the Yukon looking at the trailer wheels spinning we saw a pickup truck come around the same hill and go into a fishtail and almost hit our wreck. The truck just nicked our upside down camper. When we saw this about to happen Wally ran for the woods and I just stood there frozen like a fool—but Lucky Pierre (me) was lucky.

We righted the trailer and limped into a gas station on mile 777.7. Here we repaired our trailer paid $2.00 for repairs and left looking very ragged. (we heated the hitch and turned it around).

We drove into White Horse and here tuned up our V.W.

As we drove toward Prince George in a gas station I noticed that our wheel bearings were gone on the trailer so we spent the remainder of the day working on the bearings and the V.W.

7/7/68 Prince George, B.C. Area Rain and some sun today, very scenic drive along the Thompson River and Fraser Valley.

Lucky Pierre has a new nickname "Skunk"

Wally at knifepoint thinks Alice is nice.

Little dirty Dick Dawson felt rapport with two waitresses similar to Lucky Pierre's Alice.

I carved a statue from a piece of horn I had found.

Crossing the border back into Canada was a big nothing. There was no one at the border. I still had my Luger pistol under the seat and no one told me to put it into a plastic bag.

Dawson was a half ghost town, so many buildings empty, so little life force in the whole town. It would have been great to look for treasures and antiques in this deserted town but we just walked around.

We went on to White Horse and Robert Service cabin.

Robert Service cabin.

Walter by another tourist type cabin

Val looking for something to shoot—bear or wolf

Val with a pike at Frenchman's Lake.

Our rig the VW and our Montgomery
Ward pop up camper and me.

It was a scenic area around White Horse and we really
enjoyed the views. White Horse also had showers where we
could wash up very inexpensively. This was a big deal for
travelers like us.

Walter on not so scenic view

Walter in a more scenic setting.

The drive between Dawson and White Horse was scenic but most of all it was so desolate, like nothing is there. When city people like us end up in a land of no people roads, buildings we get an effect of complete freedom. There seemed no restraints on us.

From Dawson we drove toward Carmacks. There was nothing but mountains, forests and the sky. We saw some game along the way, mostly moose.

Cow Moose

Val and the huge emptiness and a feeling of being totally free

----50 years later how I remember the Carmacks story

One of our adventures started around Carmacks. Driving in the mountains we taught that coasting down hill we could save gas and make it to Carmacks, but that did not work out and we ran out of gas a few miles before Carmacks. Walter who had been driving for a long time was tired and needed sleep, so... it was up to me to walk through the mountains and bring back some gasoline. I walked and walked for a long time and finally reached the small town of Carmacks, Yukon.

Carmacks is a community in the **Yukon** with about 500 year-round residents. Visitor services include hotel rooms, a service station, a convenience and grocery
(this information was on the internet)...

So there I was in Carmacks at the service station, dirty, tired of walking and here I met a female attendant Alice. She could not believe I walked out of the mountains trying to get gas. She was funny and friendly, somewhat heavy but I did not care, she was a girl. You can see where my mind is going. She managed to find some bottle, cans to give me about a gallon of gas I could carry back to our VW.

The girl at the gas station seemed to like me and we had a sort of immediate rapport. This was very strange or maybe I was just starved for female attention.

I walked back to the car with the gasoline and told Wally that I met this girl, Alice and that we can go camping at Frenchman's Lake and catch a lot of pike. We were able to drive into Carmacks and I introduced Wally to Alice who also introduced us to Lynn a friend of hers who also worked in town. We bought gas and some supplies and set up an evening date with the two girls by the lake. A dream come true for two very horny guys.

My diary explains that we fished a lot, partied a lot, smoked a lot of pot and sat around a fire, Alice played with her guitar, it was a great evening after evening by the beautiful lake. After drinking and smoking we all went to bed in our camper, and the fun continued.

Val I still looked civilized

During our pot party in the camper I wanted to play the bad wolfman and entertain the girls.

Val entertains girls as the wolfman

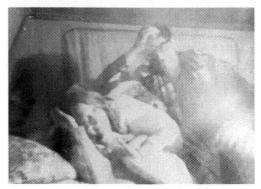

bad photo of Alice and Val

The campground at Frenchman's Lake provided us with a break from our travels.

Wally with a bunch of pike he caught

Wally and Lynn during one of our parties in the camper.

Wally and Lynn getting ready to party

Lynn with a pike she caught

Two other interesting things happened at this campground while we fished and partied. We were constantly visited by a black bear and we fed the bear with the guts of the pike we caught, the bear got used to the feedings and kept coming around every day. We being smart and clever decided to make an 8mm film of me shooting the bear with my bow, Wally backing me up with a gun. What a great stupid idea that was.

Val checking out his arrow by the camper.

Wally with rifle ready to back me up

We had found what we believed some grizzly bear tracks around the camp, so when I was alone in camp I always carried shotgun loaded with buck shot. One afternoon Wally left to pick up the girls and I decided to wash up in the lake. I undressed and took my soap and shotgun to the lake shore when I suddenly saw the black bear coming into our camp. I fired one shot to scare it away but it was hungry and was not frightened away. I backed into the lake about four feet of water and tried to go along the shore away from the bear.

I think I had four more shells in the gun so I knew I could blind or kill the bear with that much buck shot. The bear paralleled me along the shore. I hoped Wally would soon return with the girls and scare the bear away.

I began to count to a hundred as I was beginning to get very cold but the bear just sat on the shore line looking at me. I would start walking to the right so would the bear. I began to think that a some point I would have to blast the bear in the head. I then taught that Wally would think I took the bear to have the hide all to myself, so I counted to another hundred and got colder and colder.

I could not believe it took so long for Wally to pick up the girls and come back from Carmacks. I was so cold that I decided to blast that bear when suddenly I heard the VW come driving into camp, I was saved, the bear walked away.

In my diary I mention the Canadian police and game warden came to see us in camp. They were confused about us they could not believe poor hippy type characters had such an amount of material goods. The best guns, cameras and other things. They asked to see if Wally could shoot good, and he did show them by hitting some targets.

They also told us that the black bear could have torn me to pieces in a few seconds in the water if it wanted to do it. They also told us it was illegal to shoot the bear and make a movie. We could only kill the bear if it attacked us.

So...they could not find anything to arrest us for or fine us for and they could not understand that we were just simply looking for adventure and enjoyed camping out with the girls. Their solution to us was to suggest very politely that we would be better off if we just left the area as soon as possible. There was no reason given but the fact was that we were an enigma to the society they represented. We were neither crazy hippies, crazy anarchists, bandits, hermit types we were normal people taking a brake from living a standard civilized life, people like us pose the biggest scare to the plebian working drones who are afraid that more people will start looking for freedom and upset their world.

So…we left our great campsite, the two girls, our constant companion the black bear and headed out to Prince George and then to the border and into Seattle Washington.

7/8/68
Seattle, Washington and California bound

Warm 75%, sunny
Visited Denny's Restaurant—Wally called his broker and bought some stock
We took showers and washed our clothes at the Rogue River Valley Camp. Here I also called my friends the three French nurses in San Francisco. I have great expectations.
Mileage at night was 44921

7/9/68
California---San Francisco

Sunny-warm
With great expectations of the French girls we pushed south toward San Francisco from the Rogue River Valley.
It took us a longer time than expected to reach San Francisco, so I called the girls and told them we would be late.
We pulled into the San Francisco area about 10:00 PM and went to the Sam Taylor Park but found it filled so we left our trailer there and drove to see the French girls
We bought them a bottle of brandy and a bottle of wine, I also gave them three little presents of 1 fossil, 2 sketches,3 Eskimo calendar.
To say the least they were surprised to see us and our condition.

Here we came dirty as mother fuckers, bearded, tired and overall looking like two turds with stinking feet.

Good old European hospitality---they gave us food and talked to us.

My mind was set on sex because a man can not live on Alice alone.

So as we retired, I on the floor, and Wally on the couch—I made my play. I walked into Odette's room sat down on her bed and placed my hand on her ass.

The response was not good, so I like a gentleman left to lay down on the floor.

The light went out as I lay there on the floor I taught that perhaps Christiane was horny for my body—so I knocked on her bedroom door and asked her for a blanket, then I made my play and got refused again, but managed to get a kiss for all my troubles.

7/10/68
San Francisco

Weather....fine

(I would also like to remind the reader that this time the VW could only start with a push).

Got up in the morning and fixed pancakes for Paula and Christiane and went back to sleep.

All three of us got up late and went sightseeing with Odette Saw some hippies and went to a park where we saw elk and buffalo.

Later all three of us walked on the beech.

We went back to the Sam Taylor Park but it was filled again so we picked up our trailer and bought 2 new tires, we also had our first Orange Julius at this time.

53

In the evening we went out with Paula and checked out the hippy district, as we walked we were offered LSD, hash, pot. We stopped by in a few shops and I bought Paula a trick Turkish ring.

When we went home I tried to make out with Odette---she let me kiss her and feel her breasts, but would not respond at all, then she told me that what I wanted was a woman---any woman and was not interested in her as an individual. She was mad at me and we went to sleep.

P.S. while in the district a nigger hippy ran up to us and told us the world was ending.
P.S.S. Odette was very embarrassed to be seen with us.

7/11/68
San Francisco

Weather---warm
In the morning had a nice conversation with Christiane and then went to the Haight -- Ashbury Dist.

Val and Odette in San Francisco

Street view of Haight---Ashbury Dist

Wally and Odette in San Francisco

Street scene Haight-Ashbury

Looking from a bistro at the Haight-Ashbury.

Wally in a poster shop in Haight-Ashbury

Val in the same poster shop in Haight-Ashbury posing under a horse's ass

Haight-Ashbury - Wikipedia
https://en.wikipedia.org › wiki › Haight-Ashbury

Jump to Geographic situation within **San Francisco - Haight-Ashbury** is a **district of San Francisco**, California, named for the intersection of **Haight** and **Ashbury** streets. It is also called The **Haight** and The Upper **Haight**. The neighborhood is known for having been the birthplace of the hippie counterculture of the 1960s.

While driving Wally picked up two hippy girls, Susan and Mary-Beth, they were from the east coast. We bought them breakfast and told them to meet us at 6 pm by our car. I told Wally not to sweat the pussy situation---we will find a cook that wants to fuck and go to Mexico with us.

As we started our walk in the district we met a girl with a baby. This hippy girl wanted to come with us—but we did not know what to do with the baby. Other hippies approached us and tried to sell us pot and other drugs.

We tried to take a piss in a Standard Gas Station---but they would not let us---so we pissed in the park.

In the district we ran into a group of hippies that we fooled around with. I took some pictures of them and Wally the piker managed to mooch some chocolate cake from them.

Wally sitting down with hippie group and eating chocolate cake

Same hippie group, two of the males feeling up the hippie girls

On this day we also bought some posters. In one walk through the Ashbury district we met a blonde, blue eyed male hippie---who after I asked him where we could get some ass— rolled his mouth at me, told me he had the standard equipment and was willing to take a gram from me.

We also met a demented woman that ripped our sign "Make Love Not War" in half.

Before we left that night we met three hippie girls, very young, who wanted to go with us---they did not want to split up. I had very great hots for one of them---a little blonde.

This night we left S.F. and went south. We slept in an apricot orchard.

P.S. I think Paula would have fucked us.

The 50 year old diary gives us a then perspective of a reality at that time. Today 50 years later I see that old reality in a different light.

1. Our expectations of a lot of sex from the three French nurses were unreal. They saw us almost as hobos, dirty, horny, unemployed…why should they take up with us? They had good husband prospects in the hospitals they worked in. Today I am surprised they were so nice to take us in and show us S.F. Today I thank you girls from the past for being so nice to us.

2. I was smitten by Odette, she had a great body and was not cold, cold, completely

3. The trip trough the Ashbury district was a real eye opener to a couple of normal working people, us. The hippies were every where…absolutely beautiful hippy girls. Teeny boppers those we saw as very young were all over the place. Their dress was outlandish for guys and girls.

4. Our first encounter with a gay guy, at that time we considered a queer, surprised and confused us. We had never been propositioned by a man before.

5. The stores were full of dope type stuff, pipes, cigarette papers, posters advertising pot, freedom, love. The people were the most fantastic sight.

6. We stopped and interacted with a very interesting group of hippies; please see pictures 61, 62. This group of guys and girls was what today we believe the Manson group of killers. Manson was there in Ashbury at the time. Please see picture 61 and look at the guy sitting on the left side of Wally and through simple facial recognition we can see it is, we believe, Bobby Beausoleil, one of the killers for Manson. Believe it or not we think that is a possibility.

I believe we took highway 101 south to the LA area. During our journey we picked up a hippie girl wanting a ride. She was from the Mount Shasta area. She invited us to see her commune of hippies living in the wild hill area. The hippies lived in the wilderness in huts and tents. The girls were beautiful and the atmosphere was fantastic. There were people doing their own thing... playing beautiful flute melodies in the hills...this was very impressive to me.

As we got to know them we got invited to an ocean beach house that some very rich person let the hippies use. The house was built on a cliff that touched the ocean, it was a fantastic sight. The girl showed us the house, I was impressed...the bedroom had a ceiling that was open to the sky so if you were in bed you could look up at the stars. The other interesting place was the bathroom with a glass floor that you could look down and see the surf breaking on the rocks below while you sat on the pot.

I wish I would have gathered more information about the ownership and location of the house on the cliff.

We left the house and the hippie commune and headed for LA

Back to the 50 year old diary

7/12/68
On our way to Camarillo (Ray)

> *Warm*
> *Came into Ray's house.*
> *Cleaned up and tuned up the car.*
> *We are now very horny and thinking of Mexico.*
> *Wally called our friend Hank and I called my friend Jone.*
> *I felt very sick this night.*
> *To conclude the evening we went out for a pizza.*

In Camarillo our friend Hank by our car

In Camarillo by Rays house

Ray, his wife and me in his back yard in Camarillo

It was nice to find and stay with friends in Camarillo. We seemed like we were speeding through our trip and it was nice to stop. We cleaned up and organized our stuff. I think we sort of scared our friends, we looked disheveled and dirty, the car and trailer were dusty and muddy.

> *7/13/68*
> *Camarillo to Tijuana*
>
> > *Weather warm*
> > *From Camarillo all the way to Tijuana–Mexico-exotic land of beautiful, passionate women.*
> > *We parked the car on the U.S. side and walked into Tijuana (we figured we were smart–we would not get cheated) The first thing we did was jump into a cab and three minutes later we get dropped off in back of a whore house–we get taken for $2.50 apiece for the ride–the cabbie says–personal service. Two whores*

*grab us and drag us into their little rooms. We
don't like the way the whores look so we barter
with them and then run out to the bar in front
of the whore house.*

*Here we see girls dancing without any pants
on. One of them sits down on the bar in front of
the costumer and he ....*

At the bar we find two girls we like ....

*After all this we met back in the bar and
drank. Then we went another bar where more
girls with no pants were dancing.*

There is already too much pornography in our
literature so I will skip over some entries into my diary
of our adventures in these Tijuana bars. We drank and
enjoyed every bit of it. Now I will go back to the 50 year
old diary.

7/14/68 T.J.--Ensenada

*After this we went to the Tempico Bar
where I met Rosa. Here I had a great time—ran
out of money---but Rosa was great company.
Finally we left Tijuana crossed the border, drove
a few miles and camped out for the night. Wally
also met a girl here but did not hit it off, she
was very short and when they danced everyone
laughed because of the contrast.*

*This day (Sunday) we walked all the way
to the bullfights. It was a great time—the fights,
the sun, the beer, the local people and local color*

At the Bullfights

At the Bullfights

At the Bullfights

bullfight

Bullfight (best picture) the bull scores a point

Bullfight, the crowd gasps as the gored
matador is dragged off the arena

As we left I started talking to a beautiful blonde—she
talked back—but I was too timid to ask her to go drinking,
dancing. I shall forever regret this. Let this be a great
lesson to me that the timid shall only inherit shit.

In the evening we left for Ensenada where we camped
out at El Faro Beach.

At night we went into Ensenada and into the Kahlua Bar.

Here we sat down and watched a shitty show, then a girl
by the name of kitty came over. She was pretty, spoke good
English and told us that all she wanted was one cognac and
she would come to our camp and do the thing with us. Wally

did not trust her, but me—my faith in human nature cost me about $10.00. She never showed up while I waited on the beach road feeling very religious, drawing signs of life in the sand and waiting---then nothing---sleep.

7/15/68
Ensenada, El Faro Beach
Warm-Sunny

Got up in the morning and went horseback riding. One of the things I wanted to do—was ride a horse on the surf in the morning.

Wally riding by the surf in the morning

Wally riding by the surf

racing horses along the surf

Wally had the Jollies from Mexican food all day. After horseback riding I played chess with our camping Mexican neighbor. After this I went and sat around the beach fire with 3 surfers and a young girl called Michelle.

Late at night I went with one of the surfers into Ensenada and we went into Ho Sungs bar then we went to the Kahlua bar and saw a deformed acrobat do a show. I also think I saw Kitty run out from the bar.

7/16/68
Ensenada---T.J.

> *Sunny ---Warm*
> *Went horseback riding with Wally, had a very good time taking pictures and developing saddle sores from too much riding.*
>
> *We went swimming and saw a soldier calling us out of the water (he had a rifle). He only wanted to warn us of the strong undertow in the area.*
>
> *We played chess—I lost and got a big sermon from Wally on how warped my thinking is —if I think I can beat him in chess.*
>
> *We also bartered and bought a watermelon. In Ensenada I had a good time playing in the store with a Nazi helmet, I bought a chess set there.*
>
> *Left back for T.J. there is not much action in Ensenada.*
>
> *Back in T.J. we went back to the same bar and being sober I saw my girl Rosa as nothing more than an ugly "B" girl.*
>
> *We drank a little but then went over the border to set up our camper on the U.S. side in a parking lot.*

7/17/68
T.J.------LA

> *Warm ----Sunny*

VALENTINE L. KRUMPLIS

> *Went back to T.J. to shop. Wally and I met*
> *a pimp…he promised Wally a real nice girl….*
> *well he fell for the sales pitch….I censor the rest*
> *of this sordid event…it was a house wife with*
> *curlers who was cooking dinner but interrupted*
> *to entertain Wally.(Anyone interested in the real*
> *story have to ask Wally for all the details).*
> *Left T.J. and drove to Laguna Beach.*
>
> *P.S. Every time we crossed the border they asked us*
> *what we did for a living and once they frisked us.*

Fifty years ago… the memories of our Mexican adventures grow fuzzy, the diary is a big help. I do not want to quote word for word the sexual adventures in the diary because today the comments seem crude and vulgar. In summary one can say that there was a lot of sex in Mexico. There were bars with great shows, whorehouses with fifty or more girls, there were pimps on the street advertising all of that.

The other things that I remember were the dangers to the naïve visitors. We were approached several times by seedy looking lowlifes who said "Hey mon you want to see great silver works real cheap in the mountains where they work, you come with me". Yes I could see what would happen to us in the mountains to buy cheap silver trinkets. We never went anywhere with these bullshitters.

The other gimmick they constantly tried was to say to us: "Hey hippie you want to make a lot of money, we sell you real cheap marijuana, horse (heroin), you take back make a lot of money. Yep, a lot of hippies fell for this bullshit line. The sellers would then run to the border cops and point out the mules with the dope. The cops would extort money from hippies and their parents. It was interesting that a lot of hippies approached us stating this problem and asking fellow Americans, us, to help bail out their arrested friends for dope smuggling. So...in those days you had to be careful not to fall in all kinds of gimmicky shit.

In final summary to be in Mexico was great, the lovely girls, great drinks, horseback riding along the surf all of that made life a very happy adventure. Two other things made the adventure more fun: 1. having money to do all that and the time to do it. 2. being young to enjoy it to the fullest.

> *P.S.*
>
> *Every time we crossed the border they asked us what we did for a living, and once they frisked us.*
>
> *In Laguna Beach we met hippies and stayed with them "around Feed in "on the beach. We introduced our selves.*
>
> *Then I treated cheapskate to a 10 cent tram ride to the Laguna Art Festival. (Class for W.S.)*
>
> *We Ended up at Jone's (My fraternity sisters place) and found Emans there (Jone in a robe)*
>
> *We drank, talked and Emans left disappointed.*
>
> *I went to sleep in the garage, Wally slept on the couch.*

Staying at my fraternity sister's small apartment and hanging out with hippies all day and night left me no time to continue with my diary...so sorry.

Jone worked all day and Wally and I had to find all kinds of amusement until she came back and we hit the night spots with her.

We went to two Nightclubs, Pancho's and Cisco's where Jone had a tab and we drank on it.

At this time I was still suffering from saddle sores riding on the surf in Ensenada. I went to a local drugstore and told them I had saddle sores, the druggist told me no one had that problem here for a hundred years...he gave me some ointment.

We celebrated every night in the clubs or on the beach. I met another fraternity sister here, Chris, and stayed with her for a few days, she had some weird friends. I met at some parties and ended up sleeping at her black friends apartment, Cedric who was gay and really, really got to like me too much. He had a million records and wanted to play them all for me, I must have broken his heart when I told him I was only interested in girls.

One morning I woke up on the floor with Chris in Cedric's apartment and there were two big black guys with Cedric helping me off the floor...the strange moment passed and they turned out to be very nice polite people.

At another party with Chris I met A girl I had met in Chicago we were sitting around and she kept nibbling on my ear, I warned her what will happen to her right at the party...she kept nibbling.

We finally left the hippie heaven and all our friends and headed to Las Vegas for one of the last interesting events of our Alcan trip.

Las Vegas

We arrive in Las Vegas with our VW pulling our banged up dirty trailer with a bumper sticker that says "Make Love Not War". Wally and I by this time are tired and have the look of homeless people or people who live in their cars. We immediately attract the attention of the police on one of their main streets and get pulled over. We have to go through the whole series of questions to prove that we are not anarchists or vagabonds but just guys on a long vacation. Then they ask us if we have guns, yes we do a whole shitload of guns. The cop then asks me if we have handguns, yes I say I have a German 9mm Luger under the seat. The cop says can I see it, of course you can, and I reach under the seat and hand him the Luger. This is all taking place with people walking around and cars all over. The cop wants to see if the Luger is loaded but he has no idea how to open it. So...he hands the luger back and asks me to see if there is a bullet in the chamber. I open the Luger and show him it is empty. The cop now says thank you and tells me to put the Luger back under the seat.

This is what the world was in the 1960's, how beautiful and free America was.

Compare today to what the cops would have done to us for a pistol under the seat of a car. The world has changed and has changed America

Epilogue

What is it about the whole trip? It was an adventure by two young people breaking out of the roles society wanted them to play. We did something different and collected a chest full of treasures, memories that you can enjoy every day in your old age. This book is written to invite the young people to reach for the stars, do much, love much, dream much and do not fall into prescribed ruts that society wants us to follow

Printed in the United States
By Bookmasters